Renal Diet HQ IQ
Teaching You To Master Your Health

Mindful Eating For A Pre-Dialysis Kidney Diet: Healthy Attitudes Toward Food and Life

RENALDIET
HEADQUARTERS
BY HEALTHY DIET MENUS FOR YOU

Purpose and Introduction

What I have found through the emails and requests of my readers is that it is difficult to find information about a pre-dialysis kidney diet that is actionable. I want you to know that is what I intend to provide in all my books.

I wrote this book with you in mind: the person with kidney problems who does not know where to start or can't seem to get the answers that you need from other sources. This book will provide information that is applicable to a predialysis kidney disease diet.

Who am I? I am a registered dietitian in the USA who has been working with kidney patients for my entire 15 + years of experience. Find all my books on Amazon on my author page: http://www.amazon.com/Mathea-Ford/e/B008E1E7IS/

My goals are simple – to give some answers and to create an understanding of what is typical. In this series of 12 books, I will take you through the different parts of being a person with pre-dialysis kidney disease. It will not necessarily be what happens in your case, as everyone is an individual. I may simplify things in an effort to write them so that I feel you can learn the most from the information. This may mean that I don't say the exact things that your doctor would say. If you don't understand, please ask your doctor.

I want you to know, I am not a medical doctor and I am not aware of your particular condition. Information in this book is current as of publication, but may or may not have changed. This book is not meant to substitute for medical treatment for you, your friends, your caregivers, or your family members. You should not base treatment decisions solely on what is contained in this book. Develop your treatment plan with your doctors, nurses and the other medical professionals on your team. I recommend that you double-check any information with your medical team to verify if it applies to you.

In other words, I am not responsible for your medical care. I am providing this book for information and entertainment purposes, not medical diagnoses. Please consult with your doctor about any questions that you have about your particular case.

Table of Contents

What Does Mindful Mean?

What does it mean to be mindful? How do you think it feels to be acutely aware of everything you touch, see and do?

Thich Nhat Hanh, who authored "Peace is in Every Step: The Path of Mindfulness in Everyday Life", describes the concept of mindfulness in a few succinct words:

"Walk as if you are kissing the Earth with your feet."

Think about that for a moment. What if you were aware and tuned into every single step you take? What would that feel like? How would it make you feel? This is what mindfulness is. It's about being aware and completely in the moment. Now if that's not you, read on because this is part of helping you do better with your kidney disease.

In Practice

When you are mindful, you work to be aware of each thing you do. If you are practicing mindfulness in life in general, you will be aware of what you eat, but also what you are doing and how. Awareness comes with practice.

For example, if you are taking a walk, you won't just focus on the walk and how tired you are starting to feel, but you'll tune into what the leaves sound like as they crunch beneath your feet and how the cool air feels on your face. You might notice that the sky is neither blue nor white, but a mix of cloud and sky. You might stop to finger the petal on a flowering bush.

Being mindful is about being in the moment and aware of your life, of your surroundings and of what you are doing and why. Many people believe that mindfulness helps to ground you and give you a focus. They believe that when you are mindful, you are also respectful of what you have, and not focused on what you do not have.

When you practice mindfulness, you don't let a single detail that you feel, see or do pass you by unnoticed and unfelt. You give focus to the things around you. Being aware and enjoying the moment are key to your practice of mindfulness.

How Mindfulness Helps You?

As life gets increasingly busy and chaotic, it's a nice thought that we could just stop and listen, feel, and see things. Not necessarily physically or mentally but stop, and also calm your mind. Some advocates of mindfulness argue that today's busy world requires more mindfulness, not less, because of the amount of distraction we experience.

Mindfulness is based in Buddhism and is considered one of the seven components of enlightenment. Buddha said "when you maintain this calm awareness of your body and feelings, you gain wisdom." Wisdom that we probably miss in our busy lives because of how hectic life gets.

Mindfulness shares qualities with meditation. Both require you to slow down, to take a breath and to fully examine life and everything around you. You derive great benefits from both, including an ability to be in the moment and in a state of full awareness. Plus health benefits like lower blood pressure and reduced stress.

Now, it's not always easy to maintain this kind of focused awareness, so it takes practice and repeated efforts. As with anything, there's a learning curve and for some people that curve will be small and easy and for others, it will be much more of a process.

Once you begin practicing mindfulness, you might notice a few solid benefits. These include:

- **Reduced stress** – When you are actively living your life, aware of everything that is happening you are much less likely to suffer from severe stress. Your focus on the now helps you not worry about the future, but instead work on what is happening in that moment.
- **Memory improvements** – Some studies have shown that people who meditate and train themselves in being mindful experience improved memory when compared to those who don't practice mindfulness. Probably because they weren't distracted in the first place.
- **Improved relationships** – Want to have happier and more satisfying relationships? Consider learning how to be mindful in life. Several studies have confirmed that people who practice mindfulness respond better to stress in a relationship compared to people who don't have a mindful approach to life. They also have greater skill when they are communicating their emotions to a partner. Likely because they are more aware of their feelings.
- **Better control of emotions** – One study looked at people who had practiced mindfulness from one to 29 years and found that in the majority of these people, their mindfulness practice helped them disengage from emotional memories that upset them. Researchers determined that these people also likely handle the emotional stresses and triggers in their lives better than people who did not practice mindfulness.

- **Improved health** – When you live mindfully, you experience so many mental health benefits that you will generally also experience overall improved health. When you eat mindfully, you are more likely to make choices that are good for your health.

What About Habits?

As a person with kidney failure, your ability to incorporate some mindful habits will make a difference in your health. Kidney disease is a stressful and emotionally frustrating experience at times. You will be able to use some of these techniques to improve both your health and emotions. Mindful practice can be useful from the day you learn you have kidney failure because you are able to learn how to control and manage your emotions and reactions. Being mindful is not just about what you eat, but it's about the way that you live your life. Having kidney failure changes many things, but you can embrace and improve your life with mindful practice on a daily basis.

You might wonder how you change what you've been doing for so long? Our habits dictate so much of what we do. They dictate where we part our hair and where we place our keys when we get home. Whether good or bad, habits are often at the core of everything you do each day. Most habits are developed to help us do something consistently over and over again – whether it's dealing with emotion or exercising in the morning.

If you are in the habit of grabbing a donut when you arrive at work, you may think it's hard to make a conscious choice to ignore the donut and walk empty-handed to your desk instead. This is the problem with habits, we think it will be hard to break them.

Our habits give so many clues to us and the things that are important to us. When we decide to make other things important through mindful actions, it involves literally changing how we see the world. In order to do something different in how we interact with our world, making changes in our habits is one of the best things we can to do. It might be work but it's valuable to do.

The good news is that it's not impossible. If you are dedicated to it, you can act mindfully and create moments where you focus fully on the moment enough that you can also disregard a habit, no matter how long that habit has been a part of who you are. Over time these behaviors become easier and you do not find it difficult to do!

Once you learn some basic mindful living (and mindful eating) techniques, it will be easier to break habits because you won't act in a way that you have always acted; instead, there will be some considerate thought behind each action and over time you will notice that you've developed new habits. It will be a process of small changes over time that you don't even notice happening but suddenly realize you are no longer doing that activity that was detrimental to your health.

Our habits often dictate much about our diet and lead us to eat without thorough consideration. If we have done this for years, it can be extremely hard to suddenly stop eating just anything quickly and without much thought. It requires effort to create new habits, new tendencies and new focus for energies. Once you have done this, you can be well on your way to creating new habits and to learning how to eat with mindful intention.

Change Your Habits

To successfully incorporate mindful eating, you must be willing and able to change your habits. A habit is something you do almost without thinking about it. Some examples of good habits include always looking both ways before crossing the street, or always washing your hands after using the bathroom.

Our habits weren't always habits – many times we had to learn to do these things as children but as we get older, we realize they are just part of who we are.

Eating a specific way can also be considered a habit. You might sit in front of the television or computer when eating, or you might add salt to your food without tasting first. These are habits that can be broken, but when you have engaged in them for many years, a real effort must be made to change these habits.

To change your habits, do it slowly. Start with one thing. Perhaps you always salt your food. For a few days, try creating a new habit of trying the food first and making a conscious decision about whether or not the food needs salt before salting. If you determine that your food is a little bland and in need of some flavor, go ahead and add some additional flavor, such as a salt free blend seasoning. Try to identify the individual flavors that the seasoning adds.

What you have done is a simple thing, but it's all about making that mindful and thoughtful decision to focus on the food and to break a habit that might be unhealthy for you.

What is Emotional Eating?

Many of us are guilty of emotional eating at least once in a while. Some people habitually eat in this fashion, while others succumb during periods of stress or anxiety.

But what is emotional eating and how does it play into "mindful" eating?

What is Emotional Eating?

Emotional eating is nothing more than eating when you want to feel better. It has little to do with hunger or even true cravings. It has everything to do with dealing with emotions. If you feel like you have to eat something to feel better, this might be emotional eating.

Some ways you can tell if you are eating emotionally is to ask yourself a few questions:

- Did the "hunger" you are feeling come on gradually (physical hunger), or did it come on suddenly (emotional hunger)?
- Are you hungry but open to several options or are you sure that only pizza or chips will tame the hunger? When you are actually hungry, you are open to many options, but emotional hunger is often about the specific (often junk or comfort) food craving.
- Do you stop eating when you are full or do you continue eating long after you feel full? Emotional eaters will often eat well past the point of truly squelching their appetite.
- Do you feel guilty after you eat? Emotional eating will often trigger feelings of guilt, while eating for physical hunger won't.

Emotional eating can very easily be described as mindless eating. When you eat emotionally, you might give little thought to the choices you are making. In fact, after the first few potato chips or spoonfuls of ice cream, you might not taste the food much at all. You likely won't slow down enough to focus on the food and give proper **mindful** consideration to your meal or snack.

When people eat emotionally, they are often not giving a great deal of thought to what they are eating, why they are choosing a particular food, or how that food might affect them. While many people eat emotionally to celebrate life's accomplishments and good moments, many more eat emotionally in order to not feel difficult or painful things, to push down bad memories, to soothe themselves with food.

Sometimes people have a craving for a certain food and feel the need for a particular item. This can be identified as emotional eating. Perhaps some food item that you routinely deny yourself because of your kidney failure might cause you to do some emotional eating.

Maybe it goes like this – you get to a moment of weakness through being disappointed in yourself. Maybe you go to the doctor after working so hard on your diet and you find out that your labs have not improved like you had hoped. That might cause you to go on a "binge" because you feel like, well – I did my best – and it didn't work. Emotionally you are feeling down so you just go and eat some of those "forbidden" foods, foods that you would not normally eat. Perhaps a lot of high potassium fruits or vegetables that won't improve your condition. Now you feel even worse once you are done. Now what do you feel like?

Emotional Eating Gives Power to Emotions

When you eat mindlessly and make food choices based on your emotional state, you give power to those emotions. Whether the feeling is sadness, frustration, anger or even elation, you are handing power over to the emotions and letting them dictate how and what you eat.

The reality is that when you eat emotionally, you are allowing your emotions to control you. You are giving up some of your personal power to your emotions and then in turn giving up power over food. This creates a cycle that's hard to get out of. While you can feel emotions fully, you don't have to eat food to feel them.

While it's great to celebrate the good things in life and to allow yourself the luxury of mourning less-than-perfect days, you should never turn over these emotions to food. When you let the food take in the emotion, you are no longer feeling it, no longer relishing the good or allowing yourself to feel the bad. Eating mindfully, on the other hand, returns the power to you. You make conscious and informed decisions about what you eat.

Often emotional eating turns into mindless eating. For example, you might turn to ice cream when you're feeling stressed. At first, there's a mindful aspect to eating the ice cream. You smell it when you open the carton and perhaps revel in the silky feel the ice cream has under your spoon when you scoop it up. But after you have eaten a couple of bites, you no longer really taste the ice cream, no longer luxuriate in its yumminess. Now, you are eating mindlessly and out of habit. The focus is no longer on the food.

You started out mindfully acknowledging that you wanted the ice cream. But once it lost the flavor in a few bites, it would have been best to put it aside and no longer eat the rest. You had your taste and you are not nourishing your body at that point.

Why Do People Succumb to Emotional Eating?
Not everyone will eat based on emotional triggers. There are many people who are never guilty of emotional eating and will either eat less when stressed (also a problem) or they will eat normally.

Emotional eating is often based in memories. When you are feeling stressed, you might find that a particular food reminds you of good times so you gravitate toward that food so you can feel good and remember those times.

Another trigger for emotional eating is conditioning. If you once had a particular food on a particularly bad day, you might always crave that food when you're having a bad day. The day triggers a need for that particular food.

As a diabetic, a person might go for chocolate when they are feeling bad because it makes them feel a little better – so they say – but it's really not helping them to be healthier. Once you acknowledge your reason for eating, through mindfulness, you can stop and eat a little differently.

Maybe you convince yourself that you just don't have time to make a lunch every day, so you go to the fast food place or cafeteria at work and buy your lunch. You overeat and feel bad about your diet – or maybe they don't even have the food you need to eat. You might let that be a crutch to help you eat what you "want" and not what is the most healthy for your body.

Where Does Mindfulness Come in?

While many people – particularly women – are prone to emotional eating, this is not a habit that's particularly hard to break. You can do the things necessary to make a change.

Most emotional eating is also mindless eating, so the key to creating an environment where you don't literally eat your emotions is to become a mindful eater.

When you are eating in a mindful way, you ask yourself what to eat and how much. You might also examine the foods you are choosing and how and why you are choosing them. Eating mindfully naturally inhibits emotional eating because there's an element of thinking about the choices you are making. You might choose to eat, but also make a different decision about which food to eat or how to prepare it or how much you eat of it.

For example, if you are at the movies consider this:

You might decide ahead of time that you are going to enjoy candy and popcorn and become excited at the smell of butter popcorn when you reach the theatre. After some mindful consideration, you decide that what you're really after is the popcorn and you choose to forego the candy.

Because you want to eat as mindfully and carefully as you can, you also decide that you'll get a small popcorn and enjoy it thoroughly. After you apply mindful eating techniques (which we'll discuss shortly), you eat just half of the small container of popcorn, savoring each bite and regretting none of it.

How to Gain Power Over Emotions

Emotions are a part of everyday life. Most people feel a range of emotions throughout the day. But some emotions cause us to react more strongly than others. Do you ever feel upset about the fact that you have kidney failure? That it's not fair? Why me? Frustrated with your doctor who failed to tell you that you had the beginning signs of kidney failure a few years ago? Frustrated with your family that doesn't understand – or worse yet wants to tell you all about how you "should" do things? Or mad because your labs came back and weren't what you wanted? Those emotions can affect your ability to eat mindfully.

Before you can learn to eat mindfully, you have to learn how to gain power over those emotions. When you don't have power over your emotional eating, it's hard to learn how to eat mindfully and be successful at it. Instead, gaining power over your emotions gives you personal power, personal control and allows you to focus on the concepts of mindful eating more thoroughly.

Regain Power by Being Thoughtful

The first key to gaining some control over your emotions is to get in touch with them. First take a careful look at your emotions. Do you mostly feel joy, sadness, anger or something else? Only after you put a name to your emotions can you really gain control over them.

Name what you are feeling and the situation that makes you feel that way. The next time it happens, you can begin to recognize the emotion that is affecting you. Write them down in a log. The more you do this, the better your ability to get control over them and begin to eat mindfully.

Be intellectual in the process of thinking about emotions. That is, consider where your emotions come from. They don't come out of nowhere, yet it can sometimes feel that way. You might think that they just pop up, giving you a sense that you are out of control. This is when keeping a journal to identify your emotional triggers can help. Look at the chart in the back of the book to see what a recommended format for tracking your emotions, time, place, what you are eating and why can be.

Sometimes you might feel an emotion that's not something you can identify. That is, you might have a feeling of sadness or dread, but you can't identify where it came from. You only know that the feeling is real. Even if you are unsure why you have an emotion, you will still have a response to it and that response might not be healthy.

Throughout the day ask yourself how you are feeling. Check in with yourself. Are you feeling stressed? Tired? Frustrated? Elated? If it helps, write down when you feel certain emotions and consider what the triggers might be for those emotions. This can help you to manage your emotional state better and makes it less likely that they will manage or control you.

Stop and Think

You can begin to practice the concept of mindful eating by being mindful about the emotions that cause you to eat for comfort or out of frustration. Certain food cravings can indicate that they are being driven by an emotional need and not a physical hunger need. Once you have checked in with yourself periodically to assess the emotions and develop a sense of why you are feeling how you are feeling, begin to ask yourself more questions.

For example, think about what brought on a particular emotion. Consider this scenario:

You are having lunch with colleagues and during the lunch, you notice that one of your office mates has given you a dirty look. You automatically begin to wonder what you did to make her mad. You think she doesn't like you and soon you are feeling frustrated and worried. She is good friends with the boss – will she share with the boss some idea that you should be fired? Now your emotions move from frustration to worry.

Often, we leave our emotions here, to stew and fester and that can lead to emotional eating. But if you take it a step further, you can instead give some intellectual thought to your emotions. Ask yourself instead:

Why am I thinking these things? Could she have meant to give that look to someone else? Is she having a bad day? Is it possible that the look had nothing to do with me but everything to do with her and I just caught the look?

Once you examine your emotions, you might find that they are simply without merit. You might immediately feel better. Once you take the time to stop and think (to give mindful consideration to the emotions), you might find that you naturally have more control over them.

Other Techniques

There are many other techniques you can use to gain control over your emotions. Consider the following options:

Get rid of core beliefs about yourself that encourage negative emotions.

Are you wondering what core beliefs are? Think of them as the stories you tell yourself when you are challenged. Do you say "I can do this" or do you say "that's too hard for me". Those responses indicate how you see yourself in the world and how you view your abilities.

Our core beliefs about ourselves are critical to how we respond to a number of situations in our daily lives. Unfortunately, many of us have core beliefs about ourselves that are inherently false, so thinking about your core beliefs can do much to help you gain control over emotions.

One of your core beliefs, for example, might be that you are an inadequate worker, that nothing you do is right. When you get a dirty look from a colleague, then, you might immediately go to that core thought about yourself and believe that the colleague is thinking that you are an unworthy worker and that you should be fired.

But if you examine this core belief, you might realize that there is no basis for it. You find, in fact, that you regularly get accolades at your jobs and regular promotions. When you examine this core belief from a place that doesn't include irrational emotions, you might discover it's far from accurate.

Consider options before reacting.
It's easy for us to let our emotions get the best of us. Because it's an emotional response, we often respond in a way that might be less than desirable. If someone says something that you perceive as mean, you might respond with an unkind comment. If someone seems to attack your worthiness as an employee, you might respond by getting defensive or by attacking their work ethic.

A better approach is to consider the various options for your response before you respond. When you find that you are getting emotional, think about at least two different ways you can respond and choose the best one for the situation. No matter what the situation is, there are at least two viable responses, and maybe even more. Consider these ideas:

- **Choose not to react**. This can be a great response, especially if you think that someone is trying to frustrate you on purpose or trying to get a rise out of you. If you choose not to react, they will likely give up and move onto someone who will give them the reaction they are looking for.
- **Choose an opposite reaction.** That is, if you would normally have one reaction, choose to do the opposite. This can cause less stress for you and allow you to take a more reasoned approach and one that has some thought attached to it. Let's say that a co-worker says something to make you feel inadequate. If you would normally get defensive, try a different tact. You might ignore the comment or say "thanks for your feedback".
- **Remove yourself.** This is one of the best techniques for handling emotions. If you stay in a tense or elevated situation for long, you can become more and more emotional and less able to handle those emotions in a calm and controlled manner. If you can, remove yourself from situations that bring an emotional reaction from you and cause stress.
- **Manage Your Exposure To Negativity.** Maybe you stop eating in the break room where people continually complain about work. Or perhaps you are stressed about your doctor's appointments – they might feel very difficult. You can decrease stress by keeping a list of question for your doctor. Think about what part of the visit is causing stress

for you? Can you control that? If you can, think about why you are not doing something to control it or manage it better.

You might be surprised to find how easy it really is to control emotions. Once you have control of your emotions, learning how to eat mindfully becomes easier.

What is Mindful Eating?

Cultivating mindfulness means cultivating a culture of awareness. This awareness extends far beyond the dinner table, but it can certainly start there.

When you tune into your body and more fully into your world, you more fully experience that world. You feel things more and are aware of everything that goes on around you and to you. It is a way of focusing and directing your actions.

When you eat mindfully, you become more aware not just of how food tastes, but how luxurious it feels on your tongue and how colorful it looks on the plate. You hear the crunch in your mouth and see how it slices on the plate. All of this adds up to being mindfully and fully aware of your food and of what you are eating.

The Principles Behind Mindful Eating

If you have ever had a moment when you feel completely at peace, you might have a sense of what mindful eating is all about. It really is all about being in touch with your feelings, with your preferences and with what your body really wants and what will support you healthfully.

Here are some basic principles of mindful eating:

- Deliberately pay attention to food, hunger and satisfaction
- Pay attention not just to your internal needs and feelings, but also pay close attention to the external environment
- Mindfulness isn't just about what you put in your mouth; it's also about acceptance – of yourself, of what is happening, and of choices of foods

- Learn to nurture your body through the choices you make
- Choose to eat food that pleases and nourishes you
- Use all of your senses to taste and explore food
- Learn to acknowledge foods you like and those you don't like without feeling guilt
- Learn to understand physical hunger and how that is different from emotional hunger
- Awareness of the effects of eating mindlessly and emotionally
- Accept and be proud of your unique eating experiences and preferences

Be Present, Be Aware
When you learn to eat mindfully, you also learn to tune into your food. You don't turn on the television and watch the news while eating your TV dinner. You sit quietly at a table and enjoy the sound of the birds outside or the chatter of your dinner companions. You hear the knife as it slices the chicken and you enjoy the crunch of the pecans in your mouth.

There's an awareness that comes from learning to eat mindfully. You become fully aware of everything surrounding the very concept of eating. This includes the décor of the dining room, the conversation of your dinner companions and the aroma of the food. All of it works in harmony to add to the experience of eating.

Your mindfulness in eating comes long before you sit down to eat. It starts when you shop for groceries. You might focus on the bright colors in the produce section and then delight in the smells of the fresh herbs. As you move along through the store, you might choose a brand of yogurt not based just on price, but on the colors of the food and nutritional value.

When you prepare food, you will be fully present in the process, enjoying the sound of the conversations with friends, the freshness of the vegetables, and the sizzle of the pan as you brown fish fillets. All of this leads to a heightened sense of what food is about and enhances your experience eating.

The key is to be present in the moment. Nothing is done without some thought or engagement. While it does take practice, eating mindfully is as much about the process as the experience. You have to work at it to truly experience the process, but once you do the experience will be all that much better for it.

Here are some things to remember about being present and aware:

- Listen to your environment and be in the moment
- Enjoy the smells of food when cooking
- Really tune into how food tastes, how it feels on your tongue, and how it feels as you chew and swallow
- Notice how the most healthful foods are the most desirable for mindful eating; they are colorful, smell delicious and are fun to prepare and cook

Engage the Senses
When you fully engage the senses in the eating process, you nearly ensure that the effort to eat mindfully will be successful. Because when the senses are fully engaged, you naturally pay more attention to all that they are taking in.

Let's look at how you can engage the senses at mealtime:

- **Smell.** When you cook, focus on cooking foods that impart delicious-smelling odors. Think about using seasonal produce and fresh herbs. These things will naturally smell better, which makes you want to taste the food to see if the smell's promise holds true. Think about how great fresh ground coffee smells and compare that to pre-ground coffee. See and smell the difference?
- **Sight.** Set the table for dinner. Even for everyday weeknight meals, you can use a tablecloth, fabric napkins, and perhaps a centerpiece. Enjoy the pleasure that a well-set table brings you and focus on how that positively impacts your enjoyment of your meal.
- **Taste.** This is a biggie. Don't just chomp and swallow when you eat; when you engage your senses, you slow down your chewing and enjoy the process of eating a delicious, well-prepared meal. Slowing down your eating helps with portion control and weight management. When you eat more slowly, your body has time to process the food and let you know when you are satisfied. Take smaller bites, savor your foods and chew more before swallowing.
- **Sound.** How does the food sound as you chew it? Is it crunchy or soft? Does it melt in your mouth quietly or do you have to mash it in your mouth to get it to go down?

Focus on Your Eating Experience

Perhaps the single most important aspect of mindful eating is learning to focus on the food and the experience of your meal.

Think about dinner last night. Now answer these questions:

- Where did you eat?
- What was the temperature like in the room you had dinner in? Was it cold or warm?
- Was there music playing or did you have the television on?
- What was the dinner conversation about? Was there any conversation at all?
- What did your food taste like? Was it savory? Did it have a sweet flavor? Were the vegetables under or overcooked?
- Did the food have a crunchy texture or was it soft?
- Did you enjoy the food?

It's likely that the first question was easy to answer, but what about the others? Did you struggle to remember?

When you eat mindfully, you are completely focused not just on the food and the experience that food brings, but also on the experience of eating the food. Where you eat and who you eat with are nearly as important as what you choose to eat.

When you eat at fancy restaurants, you often eat more mindfully than when you are at home or in more casual restaurants. That's because high-end restaurants spend a great deal of time focusing on the décor, the atmosphere, music, seating and menu. You often respond to this focus by tuning more fully into your food. You are more likely to savor the meal, tasting each bite and talking about what you have experienced. You are more likely to eat mindfully. You expect the food to be of a high caliber and you focus your attention on appreciating it.

Do you agree that you pay more attention when you are out for a special meal at a nice restaurant? What changes about the way you act? You can recreate this every day in your home when you learn how to use mindful eating techniques. Focusing on your senses as you eat does take dedicated effort. This is not something you can do eating in a car, watching TV, or being distracted by your phone. You may have to plan some evenings in the beginning to practice your mindful eating so you can get used to how it feels to be in the moment and aware.

Using A Hunger Scale

Using a hunger scale lets you focus on how you are feeling as you eat and how satisfied you feel. It's about satisfaction as much as hunger, though you will find that as you eat more mindfully on a more regular basis, your satisfaction will increase greatly by simply engaging more fully in your meals.

Your hunger scale is nothing more than a focus on your personal hunger and how it gets satiated as you eat.

As you use a hunger scale, you'll learn how to understand the physical signs of true hunger and ignore the signs of emotional hunger. You'll quickly learn the difference because you will constantly evaluate your hunger before, during and after meals.

The hunger scale starts at 1 (for truly, ravenously hungry) to 10 (completely full and satiated).

Rate your hunger before you eat, while you are eating and after you eat. When you eat mindfully, you'll notice that your numbers will change throughout a meal.

Ideally, you'll only begin eating when you note that your hunger is at a 3 or 4; here you feel hungry but not ravenous. You'll have enough control over your hunger to use mindful eating techniques. You should stop eating when you feel like your hunger is at a 7 or 8, not when it's at a 10.

If you stop eating when you are at a 10, you are stuffed, overfull and likely ate more than you really needed to eat. This is what many of us feel like on Thanksgiving. Stop at a 7 or 8 and you will stop when you are healthfully full, or just perfectly satiated. And with mindful eating, you might take longer to eat but not eat as much because your body has time to sense its fullness. In order to rate hunger, you have to stop and ask yourself about what each type of hunger would feel like. Over the next few weeks, you should start to be able to better define the different stages of hunger and how your body reacts.

Are you feeling hungry right now? Let's rate the hunger.

- Is your stomach growling? You might be at a 2 or so.
- Are you excited about getting to eat at your favorite restaurant? If so, your hunger might not be real hunger. You might be at a 6 or so, depending on when you last ate.
- Has it been at least a few hours since your last meal? You might be at a 2 or 3.
- Are you feeling like your blood sugar has dropped and you must eat now or you'll be sick? That is closer to a 1 on the hunger scale and not a good place to be.
- Do you want to eat because you are bored or anxious? Honestly, that hardly registers as hunger and we won't give it a rating at all. That's emotional hunger and does not give you proper cause to eat.

The key here is to be honest with yourself. Even if the food is spectacularly good, you should not be tempted to overeat. In fact, if the food is that good, your mindful eating techniques will help you greatly because you will truly savor and delight in every single bite you take, even if you take fewer bites than you normally do.

You might notice that learning to eat mindfully is about practice. It's about creating new habits. You are learning to become satisfied not by the plateful, but by the mouthful. While there are benefits to portion sizes and calorie counting, there are far greater benefits to you when you learn to eat with a focus on how you feel. You will naturally control more of your portions because you don't gobble your food down.

Practice Mindfulness

You can start practicing mindfulness today. Try this exercise today at one of your meals and see how it goes. For this fictional exercise, we will assume you are eating dinner at a restaurant.

Consider the following:

- When you enter the restaurant, what do you notice first? Is the interior colorful or sedate? Is it a loud restaurant or a quiet restaurant? Is there music playing?
- Once inside the restaurant, see if you can smell any food. Does a waiter pass you with a tray of hot food? What does it smell like? Do the smells stoke your appetite?
- As you study the menu, pay attention to a few things. First, use your sense of sight to look around the restaurant at what people are eating. Do you see anything that is very visually appealing to you and that you would enjoy eating? Think about your sense of hearing – do you hear plates and glasses clink?

How about that sense of smell – do you smell food that makes you want to eat right now?

- Think about your hunger and what you would rate your hunger on a scale. Now look at the menu again. Think about how various foods will smell when they arrive at the table and how they will look on the plate. Imagine how they will taste as you eat them. Make your order based not just on your hunger scale rating but also on your senses. Consider ordering off the appetizer menu to get a small amount of something that you really want but won't feel like you have to eat the entire plate of it. Some restaurants offer single item orders as well.
- Think about that bread basket. Do you really want a piece of that bread? If it looks good, think about how it will taste and then decide if you must have a piece. If you do, eat it slowly and enjoy the sensation of the crusty bread in your mouth. Eat small pieces and savor them so your small piece of bread lasts. If you are not interested in the bread but want to avoid the temptation, ask that the basket be removed. If you are hungry, drink some more water. Don't mindlessly eat the appetizer.
- When your food arrives, take a moment (no matter how hungry you are) to look at it and enjoy how the chef has arranged the plate. Smell the food. Allow all of your senses to be engaged as you begin eating the food.
- Don't forget to pay attention to the little details, like how the first bite tastes or what the fish sounds like as you poke into it with your fork. Chew slowly and carefully and enjoy the feel of the food in your mouth.

- Put your fork down and ask for a to-go container when you are full.

After this exercise, think about how you normally eat. Do you hunker down and start eating the second the plate hits the table, even if the waiter warns you that the plate is hot? Do you taste a little of everything before diving in and scarfing down your food? Aside from taking a drink or chatting with your companion, do you ever stop eating long enough to examine your hunger and satisfaction level until your food is gone?

Here is another exercise:

Now try this simple exercise the next time you eat a homemade lunch at your desk.

- Place your lunch containers on your desk and open them so you can look at and savor the smell of your food. Did you pack colorful greens and a savory smelling entrée? Do you have a plate to use to display your meal?
- Focus on the environment at your desk. What do you hear right now? How does the food look to you? If it helps and if you can, put some music on so you can enjoy your food without the sound of work distractions. Can you close your door? Or eat outside on a nice day?
- Now examine your hunger. Are you at a 3 or 4? That's perfect. You are ready to eat but not so ravenous that you'll devour your meal in one swallow.
- As you eat, focus on the sensation of the food in your mouth. Even if you are eating with a plastic fork and out of a plastic container, think about how the food

looks in the container and how it tastes coming off the fork. Savor the taste of your homemade and healthy food and think about how it's nourishing your body with every bite.

- Enjoy each bite but as you work through your meal, constantly ask yourself about your hunger. Are you satisfied? Do you need more food to feel satisfied or are you about ready to stop eating?
- Once you believe your hunger is at a 7 or 8, stop eating. Sit quietly for a moment and enjoy the feel of being completely satisfied but not completely stuffed with food.

Forbidden Foods

Do you often find yourself wanting some of the "forbidden" foods that you have been denying yourself since you started on a renal meal plan? Can you think of a way to mindfully incorporate them into your eating plan?

Can you have a few bites of potato without eating it all? Do your core beliefs tell you to clean your plate? Can you see how that might not help you be a mindful eater? You could start with less and feel "ok" even if you don't eat it all. I realize this may be wasteful to you, but fix a small amount instead of the entire serving, or freeze part of the serving so you can taste a little and save it for later. Those are some ideas about how you can incorporate those foods that you feel you cannot eat into your diet. Small amounts of those foods are ok, just not very much or very often.

Incorporating Mindful Eating

While it does require thought, incorporating mindful eating into your daily life isn't difficult. There are some principles you can use that will help you train yourself to eat in a way that is mindful, appreciative, and respectful of your body. Your physical and mental health will improve.

Five Sound Principles

If you follow the basic five principles below, you'll be well on your way to learning how to incorporate mindful eating into your daily repertoire.

1. Eat only when hungry

Sounds practical, doesn't it? Yet many of us eat for other reasons, including helping us cope emotionally. If you focus on hunger (don't forget the hunger scale), you will learn to eat only when you feel true hunger; this is not the same as having a desire to eat. It's all about learning how to feel that hunger honestly. It's also not about eating because it's time to eat. You might find it easier to eat smaller meals or eat earlier in the day.

Another way to ensure you don't eat too much is to use smaller plates than the usual size of 9 inches. A small portion looks bigger on a smaller plate, and you feel like you ate a full plate of food. It's a trick of your vision, and you know it's a smaller plate but it works.

2. Allow cravings, but within reason

Eating in a mindful fashion is not about deprivation. It's more about learning how to listen to your body and enjoy the experience of eating. That often leads people down a path of eating healthfully and well. But that doesn't mean you won't have honest cravings now and then. If you feel that you must have chocolate, let yourself have a mindful dose of chocolate.

The key to having that chocolate is to get very good chocolate and enjoy the sensation of eating it. Instead of just stuffing it down, savor the way the chocolate looks and the way it feels in your hand. Smell the chocolate and then savor every creamy morsel. Eat just a serving and enjoy the feeling of satisfying a craving but in a controlled and mannerly way. Put the rest away for another day.

3. Enjoy distraction-free eating

It's hard to eat mindfully when there are noises all around you. If you normally eat in front of the computer or in your car, it's time to stop that. Instead, sit down at a table and enjoy the experience of eating as much as the food itself. Focus on the food and the experience of eating and enjoying the food. Get a plate and eat slowly and enjoy.

4. Engage all of your senses when eating

Don't forget to use all five senses when eating. You should focus on how food smells and how it looks. An important component of eating is, of course, the taste, so focus on that and enjoy the flavor burst in your mouth. Finally, don't overlook your sense of hearing or your sense of touch; both of these play a critical role in the enjoyment of food.

Another way to engage your sense of sight is to use white plates. While colorful food is an excellent way to enjoy what you are eating, when you put it against a white background you are giving it a simple way to stand out. Colors pop and provide visual appeal.

5. Stop eating when full

The most beneficial aspect of mindful eating is learning to stop eating when you're full. Using the hunger scale, be honest with yourself and assess how you are feeling as you eat. When you feel like you are nearing a 7 on the hunger scale, consider that it might be near time to stop eating. Don't exceed an 8 because this means you'll likely overeat. If you have extra food, save it for later.

One trick you can employ is the trick of putting down your fork between bites. It does take longer to eat this way, but it also allows you to be more in tune to the feeling of fullness, making it more likely you'll be able to recognize when you've had enough and make a good decision about when it's time to stop eating.

Changing Your Diet

While you can eat a Big Mac mindfully, that's hardly the purpose behind mindful eating. Part of mindful eating is being aware of how food tastes as it goes down and how you feel after you eat. While you might be able to eat a Big Mac with mindful intention, you won't get the feel-good benefits that come from having eaten a healthy, vibrantly colored and delicious meal.

When you begin to eat mindfully remember to pay attention to your renal diet. Give careful thought and consideration to the kinds of changes you could be making. Mindful eating can be a wonderful way to learn to enjoy eating smaller portions of meats and other proteins. You can buy higher quality meat products but smaller amounts and savor them at your meal. While you might spend the same amount on the meat, you can have a tastier experience with the higher quality product.

The same goes for high potassium or phosphorus vegetables. If you really want a vegetable that is high in potassium, like spinach, you could eat a small amount of it and experience every bite fully through using the mindful principles. Place a few bites of them on a plate with your other food and eat them first so you can taste them before your other foods. That process gives you the chance to eat the foods you might want some of without guilt.

When you look at your plate, you want to see a variety of colors and textures. Fresh fruits and vegetables will bring vibrant color and flavor while high-quality grains, meats, and legumes will add protein and texture. Don't forget other healthy basics as part of your diet.

Because mindful eating allows you to enjoy foods without guilt, don't buy and try to prepare foods you simply don't like. This will only cause frustration and make you feel like a failure when you end up with a refrigerator full of food you are not eating. You can try new foods, but if you know they are not something you like, don't buy it.

Instead, focus on the healthy foods that you do enjoy. Think about how you feel when you're eating them and how they look on a plate. Focus on how enjoyable they are to eat (because of flavor, texture or some other factor) and make those foods the staple of your diet. As you eat healthy more often, you might discover new foods that you love that also bring you pleasure when you eat them.

What Does it Mean to Savor?

When we say "savor" your food, what does that really mean? If you are unaccustomed to eating in any mindful fashion, the idea that you can savor your food might be a foreign one.

When you savor your food, you chew slowly and focus on the flavor, texture and aroma of the food. You notice how it feels when you cut into it and how it looks on the fork. You pay close attention to the taste and how it goes down your throat. You take your time taking another bite because you want to savor the bite before and not let it get pushed aside by the next bite.

When you savor your food, you generally eat slower and more carefully than when you eat simply to quiet a rumbling belly. There's a focused attention on the food and on the experience you have while eating the food.

Social Situations and You
If you often find yourself in social situations at mealtime you might wonder how you can eat mindfully when there are many people around, many food options and perhaps a lot of noise and distractions.

Here are some tips for mindful eating in these situations:

- Drink a large glass of water before you get to the party or social situation so you aren't ravenous when you get there
- Constantly ask yourself if you are feeling legitimately hungry in the tummy or if you just want to munch
- If you are tempted to munch and don't want to have to give that up, choose bright foods like carrots and peppers and dip those in hummus; you will have eaten healthfully but in a manner that engages your mind and focus
- Talk with yourself internally while you eat – ask yourself how things taste, how they feel on the tongue and if you like the food. If you are talking to others, put your plate down until you can focus on

the food again. Drink water or a clear beverage while you are listening.

- Use a tiny plate and go back to the buffet table only if you really want more
- In some situations it might be good to take your own favorite dish to share – like a potluck; bring something you love and that's healthy and enjoy it if there are no other solid options
- Knowing you are on a renal diet, stick to your low potassium and phosphorus foods so that eating is not a stressor.
- Stand away from the buffet table or food area so you can keep from mindlessly picking up more servings of food. It helps you to stand or sit as far away from the food as you can so if you want another serving you have the entire walk across the room to think through it mindfully.

Some Helpful Tips

Ask yourself why you are feeling a need to eat cookies or candy. If you are frustrated or stressed, think about another way you could control or handle that stress. Can you go for a walk or other activity?

Find an alternative food. Perhaps fruit will fill the sweet need or pretzels the desire for a salty crunch.

Remind yourself that you are stronger than those emotions and that no food will help you manage or control your feelings or emotions.

Cravings are even easier to manage when you have discovered the value of mindful eating. The best and most beneficial thing you can do is to ask yourself if the craving is real. Few cravings are built from physical need; instead, they are often triggered by familiar situations or a desire to have a certain taste in the mouth.

When you have a craving, work through these questions:

- What am I craving exactly?
- Where did that craving come from?
- Will anything else work to satisfy my craving?
- If no, and I decide to eat the food, will a little bit satisfy me? Can I trust myself to eat just enough to satisfy my craving?
- If yes, will I employ mindful eating techniques when enjoying the food?
- If I decide to eat the food, do I promise that I'll disallow guilty feelings?

Sometimes cravings aren't bad. Let's say you are craving a hamburger and on a Saturday night the family decides to get hamburgers. You are a little worried, because hamburgers and fries have always been your downfall and you worry that you will go overboard.

Consider this scenario instead:

- You arrive at the burger joint, your mouth watering in anticipation. You immediately notice the smell of the burgers on the grill and you can't wait to get your mouth around one. Before you left though, you drank a glass of water so you can choose from a 3-4 hunger level on your scale.
- You look at the menu board carefully and decide to order a smaller-than-usual hamburger; you normally get a double bacon cheeseburger, but decide that you don't need all of that and you are sure that the smaller, single hamburger without cheese will do.

You opt out of ordering fries because of your renal meal plan, and know that you can eat a salad if you want more after the hamburger if you are still hungry.

- When the burger arrives, you enjoy looking at the classic nature of it. You smell it and take in the aroma with enjoyment. You decide to slice the burger in half and you start on one half. As you eat with mindful intention, you realize why you love burgers. They are delightful.
- You steal a few fries from a dinner companion's basket and continue enjoying your burger. You put the burger down between bites and really focus on the sensation of the burger in your mouth. After you have eaten half, you realize you don't want more and you wrap up the leftover for your dog.

While burgers shouldn't be on your daily menu, it is OK to enjoy them in moderation, as our fictional "you" has done here. Just make sure you savor every bite and fully engage in the process of eating that burger. Stop just when you reach satisfaction. You can enjoy the burger and a bit of fries without the guilt.

What About A Renal Diet Or Allergies?
The great thing about eating mindfully is that eating this way isn't like a diet. The objective is to eat in a way that's natural for you and to tune into your body well enough that you are keenly aware of what your body wants and what satisfies you.

Because you have kidney failure, you still have to watch the protein, salt, potassium, and phosphorus content of foods and meals. And if you have diabetes, you need to control your blood sugar. But if you want to savor a food that is high potassium, you can eat a small portion – focusing on how wonderful it is and how it tastes.

You can start by learning how to eat mindfully while obeying all your restrictions, and as you get better with it with you incorporate all your foods in smaller amounts.

Practical Tips for Increasing Awareness

Creating new habits takes time. Sometimes it can be helpful to adopt other new habits that will help support the ultimate goal.

When it comes to mindful eating, there are many habits and behaviors you can adopt that will help support your goal.

Eat What Nourishes You

Now this is a tip we can all get behind. Some "diets" tell you that you can eat what you want, but it's rarely true. That's because a calorie is a calorie and overeating is always going to create problems.

But when you eat mindfully, you truly can eat what you want. Your appetite and mind are your guides and if you are truly eating in a mindful fashion, you simply won't make many mistakes after you are good at the principles.

Even if you are a great fan of fast food now, you might find that when you eat mindfully, the fat, salt and sugar found in these foods are no longer desirable to you. Instead, the colorful vegetables of a salad might hold more allure. After you eat, you will notice that you feel lighter and more energetic than when you eat the fast food. That makes it easier to choose the healthy food next time. Because you are paying attention to how your body feels.

The advice is this: Eat what you want within your restrictions, always in moderation. If you stay tuned into and focused on mindful eating principles, the good choices will be easy to make.

Make it a Habit

No matter what your current habits are, learning to eat mindfully requires you to create new habits. You will adopt habits that include:

- Thinking carefully each time you choose a food and why you are choosing to eat at this time
- Carefully considering your food as you eat and examining how it makes you feel, how it tastes and how satisfying it is for you
- Thinking about your satisfaction level and making adjustments as you eat to suit your appetite and preferences
- Learning to choose foods that engage the senses

Learning new habits takes time, but it's certainly not impossible. Practice mindful eating techniques each day and your success level will gradually increase. Over time, the habit will become natural and you'll no longer have to consciously think about mindful eating techniques – you'll simply live them.

Mindful Grocery Shopping

Mindful eating doesn't start just when you sit down at the dinner table. It starts in the grocery store. When you are shopping, you should focus on the foods you are choosing and choose them with mindful intention. If you fill your cupboards and refrigerator with colorful foods that engage the senses, eating mindfully on a regular basis will be easier.

Here are some tips for mindful grocery shopping:

- Start first in produce and think about all the delicious possibilities there. Fill your cart only with the produce items that you like. While they are interesting looking and have a fun texture and are good for you, if you don't like Brussels sprouts, no amount of mindful eating will make you like them.

- If you have previously avoided some fruits and vegetables because you aren't sure if you would like them, pick at least one new item on each trip to the grocery store. Choose it based on color, texture or some other feature that truly engages and interests you. Make sure you take your potassium, phosphorus, and sodium levels of these foods into account.
- After you have filled your cart with lovely produce, add lean meats and fish and dairy products. Avoid packaged food, but do walk down the aisles and pick up items that look interesting and that you think will satisfy you when you eat them mindfully.
- Don't be afraid to decide that certain foods just aren't for you – you won't like everything and that's OK. When you eat with mindful intention, you should be honest about your preferences and willing to make adjustments when something isn't working.

Keeping a Journal

Keep a journal and you will discover many benefits. This isn't just about keeping a journal that records what you eat. This is about recording a number of things. A good starter form is at the back of this chapter.

When you keep a mindful eating journal, you are journaling not just what you eat but also how you felt when eating. You might discuss your emotions in the hours before you ate and you might notice a pattern of food choices that are related to emotions or other triggers.

A food journal is more than what you eat. It's an important part of discovering yourselfyou're your habits and defining hunger for you. It can help you discover foods that you like and that nourish you more than others. It could also help you try new foods and see how your body reacts to them. You could simply write down what you eat, but without the context, your food journal will be nothing more than a list of foods. Give the context, such as:

- Where you were
- What the environment was like
- What the food tasted like
- Your overall satisfaction with the meal

There are a number of benefits to keeping a journal. These include having a record of your food choices, satisfaction with food and pattern of eating. Keeping a journal will also give you a sense of control over your eating and might help you see where you are making choices that aren't ideal. Plus you can see things you enjoyed and return to that experience again.

Keep it Simple

Keep your mindful eating process simple. No matter where you are and what you are doing, try to incorporate the mindful eating principles that work for you and that are comfortable for you. But keep it simple – don't stress if you aren't fully in the moment every single moment when you are eating. Just do your best.

Mindful eating does take practice and that can take time, but ultimately this is not a difficult thing to do. Once you understand the basics of mindful eating, you'll quickly see that this is not anything that's complicated.

Celebrate Success

Part of keeping things simple is learning how to congratulate yourself when you do well. When you are focused and mindful and you have days of making good choices, celebrate this. It's likely that you will be feeling well, which is reward enough, but give yourself celebratory nods when appropriate.

While mindful eating will eventually become second nature, when you are first starting out it can take focus and sacrifice. Be willing to give yourself high fives when you do well. Some people like to reward themselves with a magazine, book, manicure or item of clothing when they do well.

Benefits of Mindful Eating

There are many great benefits to eating mindfully. Sometimes focusing on the benefits of doing anything new can help you to push through challenges.

Here are some noted benefits of eating mindfully:

- You are likely to eat more healthfully since you are carefully considering everything you eat
- You learn to savor food and maybe try foods you haven't tried before
- You learn to enjoy smaller portions of food
- Emotional eating is no longer a problem
- You reduce stress
- You enjoy life more because mindful eating gives you the ability to be in the moment all the time, not just at mealtime

Learn To Be In The Moment

To be successful at mindful eating, you have to learn to be in the moment. This means learning to shut off distractions at mealtime and really focus on the moment at hand.

Many people are guilty of multitasking while eating. We text and read emails, watch the news and read magazines. We stuff in our food and walk away, never realizing that we paid little attention to the meal and gave little thought to it.

While it might be a hard habit to break, work to break the habit of doing other things during mealtime. You can't be fully present, fully aware and fully engaged in your meal if you are doing other things.

When you are focused on things other than being present and enjoying your meal, you are more likely to overeat. In order to be successful at mindful eating, it's critical that you learn to eat without distraction.

Acceptance (Self and Body)

Accept that you have kidney failure, and it's something you have to live with and be aware of. But don't let it define who you are.

Learn to accept yourself for who you are. When you are mindful in life and with food, you learn that you have to accept and be happy with what you have and who you are in order to be content. When you are living mindfully, you might desire change and work toward that, but you find acceptance in your daily existence and with your body as provided to you right now.

The interesting thing about acceptance is that many people find they are easier able to eat mindfully and with full focus when they stop fighting their body image. When they give in and accept who they are without reservation and without judgment, they begin to relax into themselves and their lives. This helps them to live more contentedly.

And a side benefit is that acceptance often brings unexpected results. People who accept themselves for who they are more likely to lose weight and become healthy than those who are struggling.

Date	Time	Place/Food	Emotion/Feeling	What/Why?
Ex: Jan 2, 13	6:30 am	Kitchen, breakfast – ½ bagel with cream cheese, water	Hungry – stomach rumbling	Eat small breakfast with meds, hungry, bagel is filling

Next Steps

1. Take the journal and start documenting your food. Know what you eat for the next few days.
2. Choose a meal to eat mindfully every day – when you have some more time to make the effort to be mindful and experience the meal.
3. If you have some foods you really want to eat but deny yourself, can you try to eat them mindfully in a small amount that will let you have the taste without the excess?
4. Expand your mindful eating practice to another meal once you are doing well with one meal.

Congratulations! You can build on your success in small bites by being mindful – but it takes a bit of time. Keep working on it.

Made in the USA
Middletown, DE
07 January 2020